Letters to My Child

Written by Amy Shipley
Illustrated by Krystal Gannon

Letters to My Child

A Children's Book About How Babies Grow

Dedicated to mothers
on the beautiful journey of pregnancy,
and to my first child.

My Child,

I'm writing to you even though you don't exist yet, but I'm ready to meet you when the time is right. I've realized there is a deeper kind of love I want to experience—the love of a child.

Love, Mom

You are ready to become the size of a tiny poppy seed.

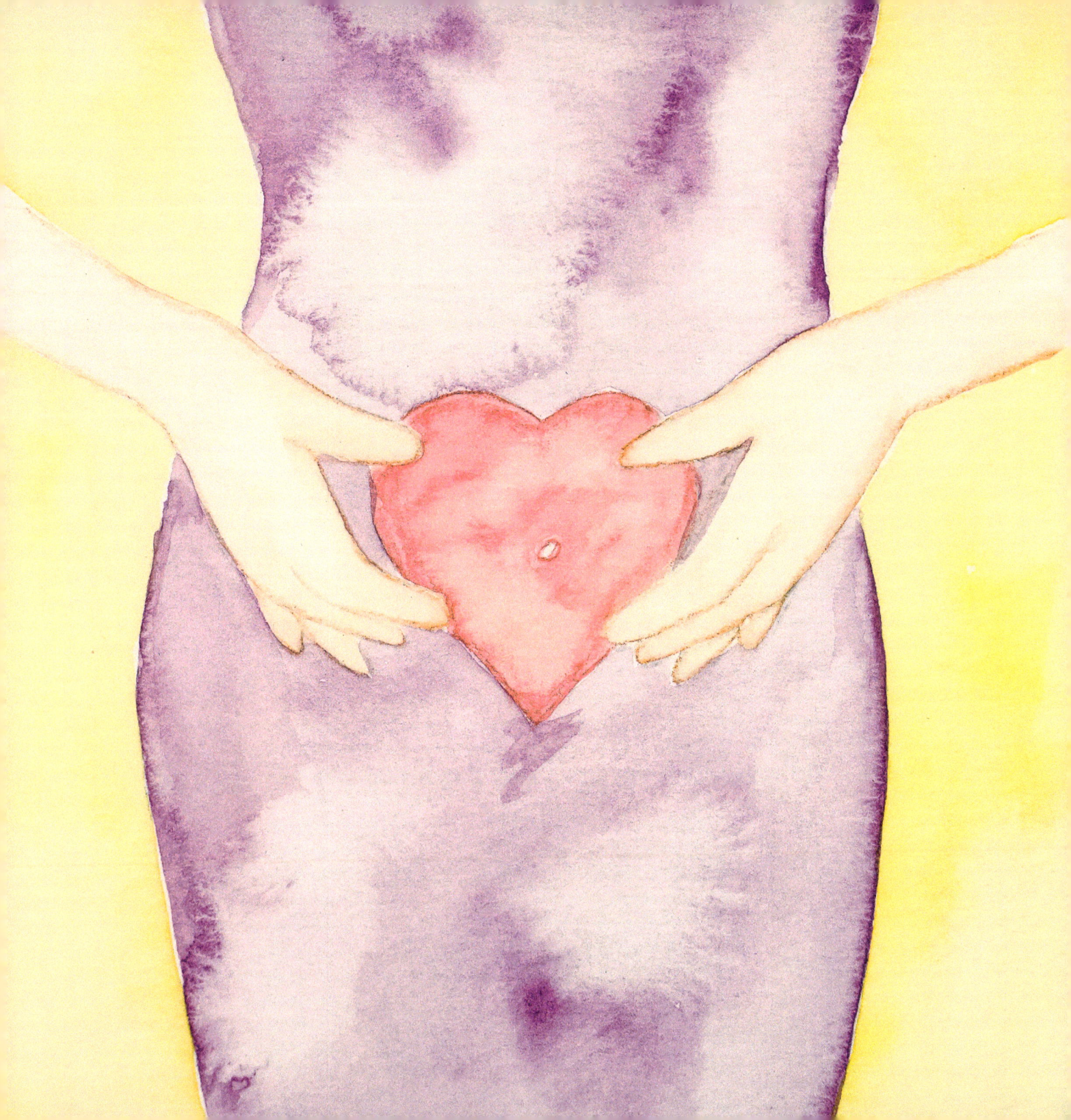

My Child,
We found out we are pregnant
with you! I just can't stop smiling.
I'm so excited, I sing and dance
around the house with you. Daddy
already talks to you in my belly;
it makes me laugh.

Love, Mom

Right now you are just the size of a tiny blueberry.

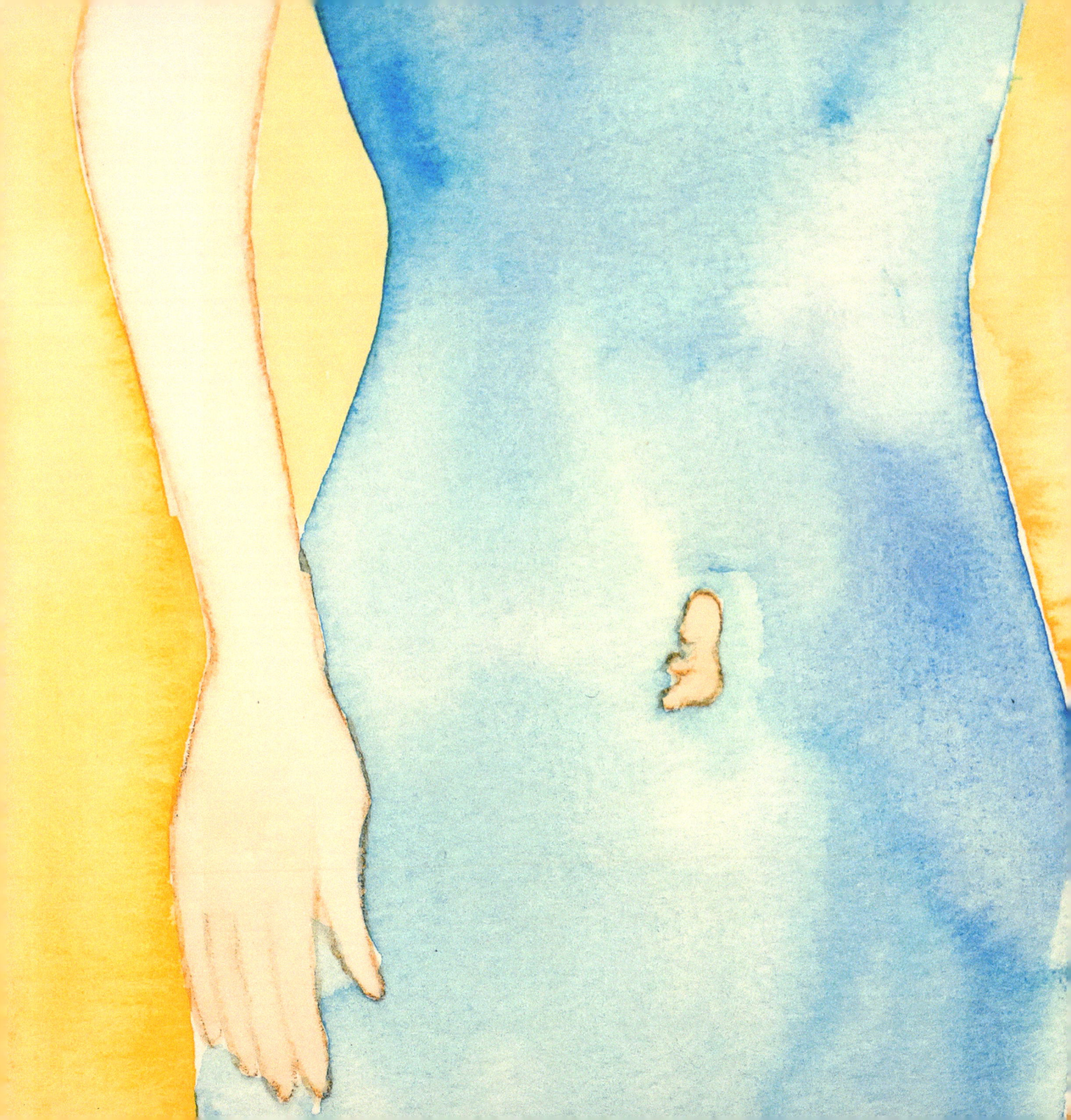

My Child,
We saw you on the ultrasound. I
can't wait to hold you. I already
love you so much. Just knowing
you'll be in my arms one day
makes me want to be a better
person, so I can be the best mom
for you.

Love, Mom

You are just the size of a little tomato.

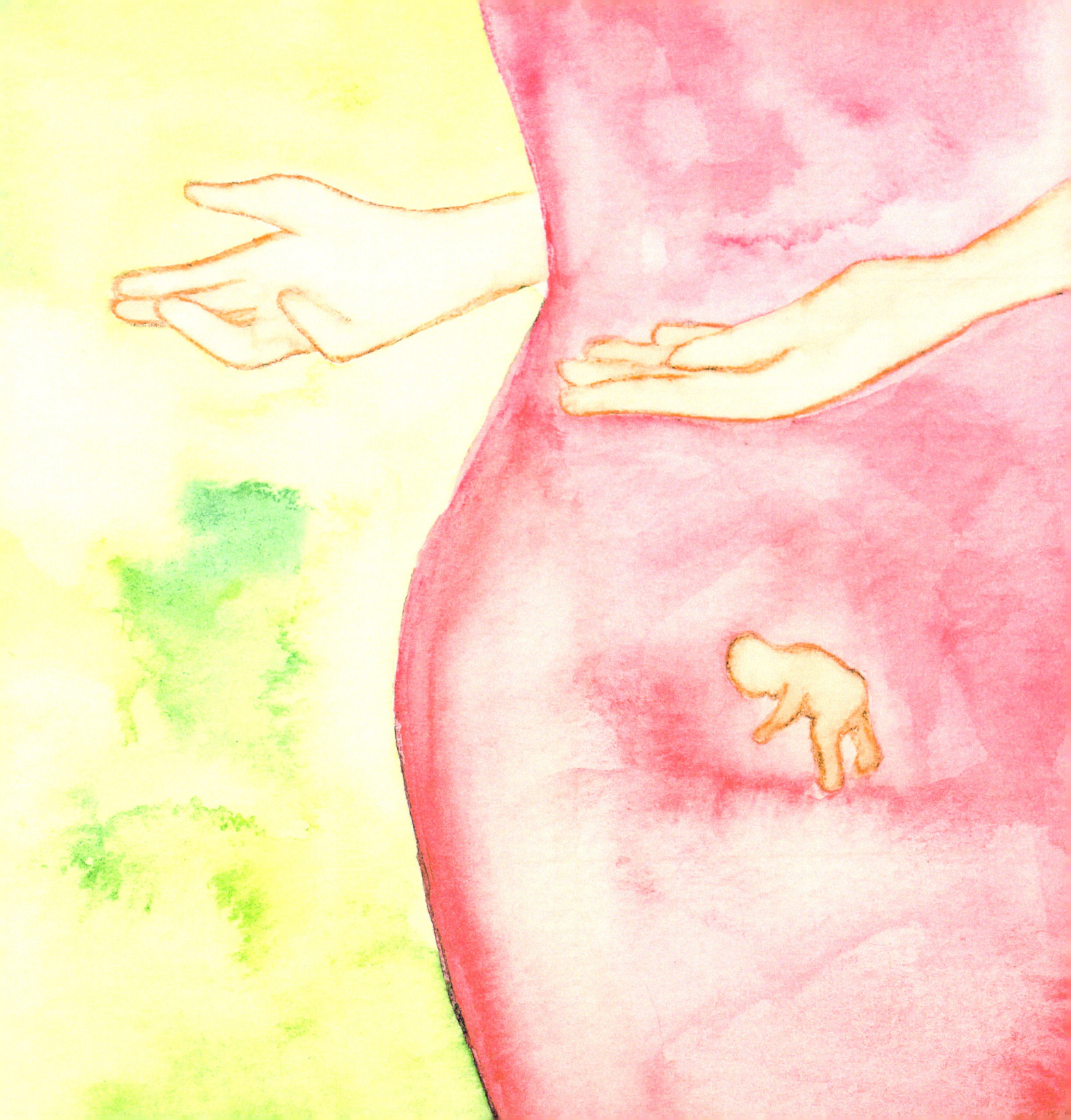

My Child,
I see a part of you in every
child I play with and hold, and I
imagine it is me and you.
I'm ready for your cuddles and
hugs. I know there will be hard
days too, but that won't stop
my love—nothing will.

Love, Mom

Now you're the size of a long banana.

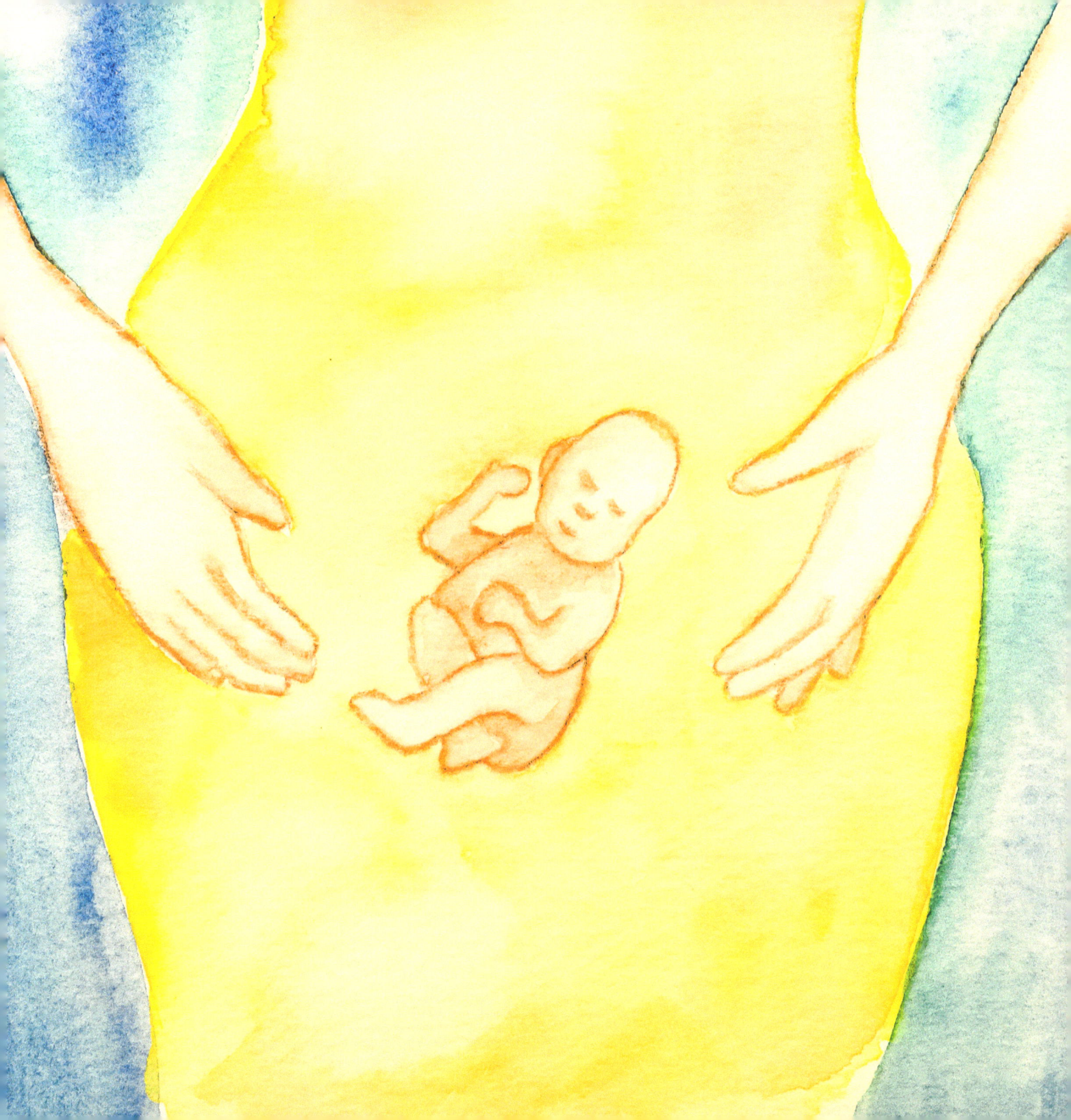

My Child,

You're so squirmy in my belly that Daddy can see and feel your little kicks too. He likes to give you a gentle push and feel you push back. I love having you in my belly because you're with me wherever I go. Keep on growing, see you soon!

Love, Mom

You are the size of a small watermelon, now.

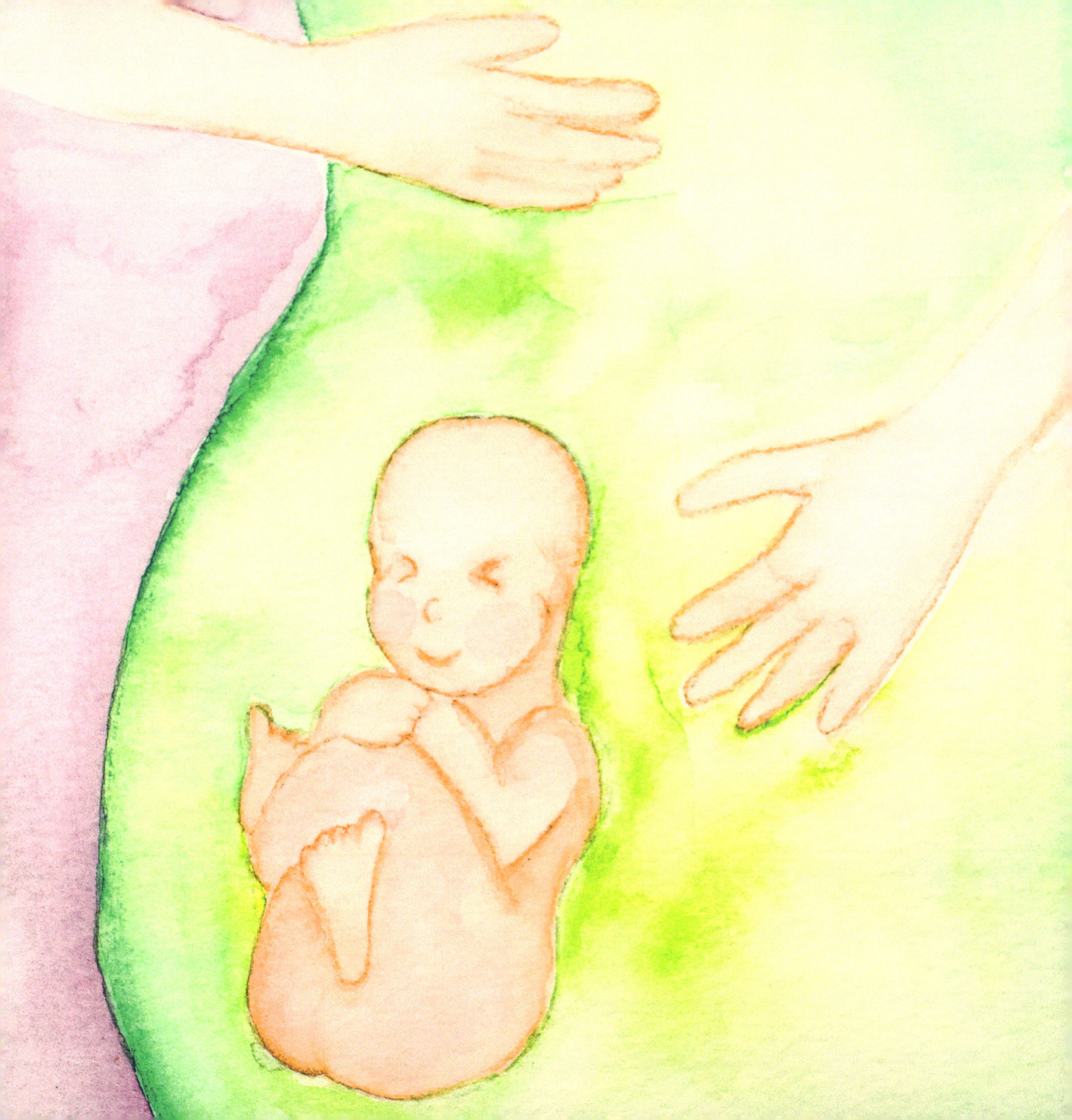

My Child,

You're finally here in my arms!
The most amazing moment was
watching your daddy talk to
you for the very first time. Now,
instead of just feeling your
hiccups, I get to see them too. It
feels amazing to be your mom.

Love, Mom

You are now the perfect size for my arms to hold.

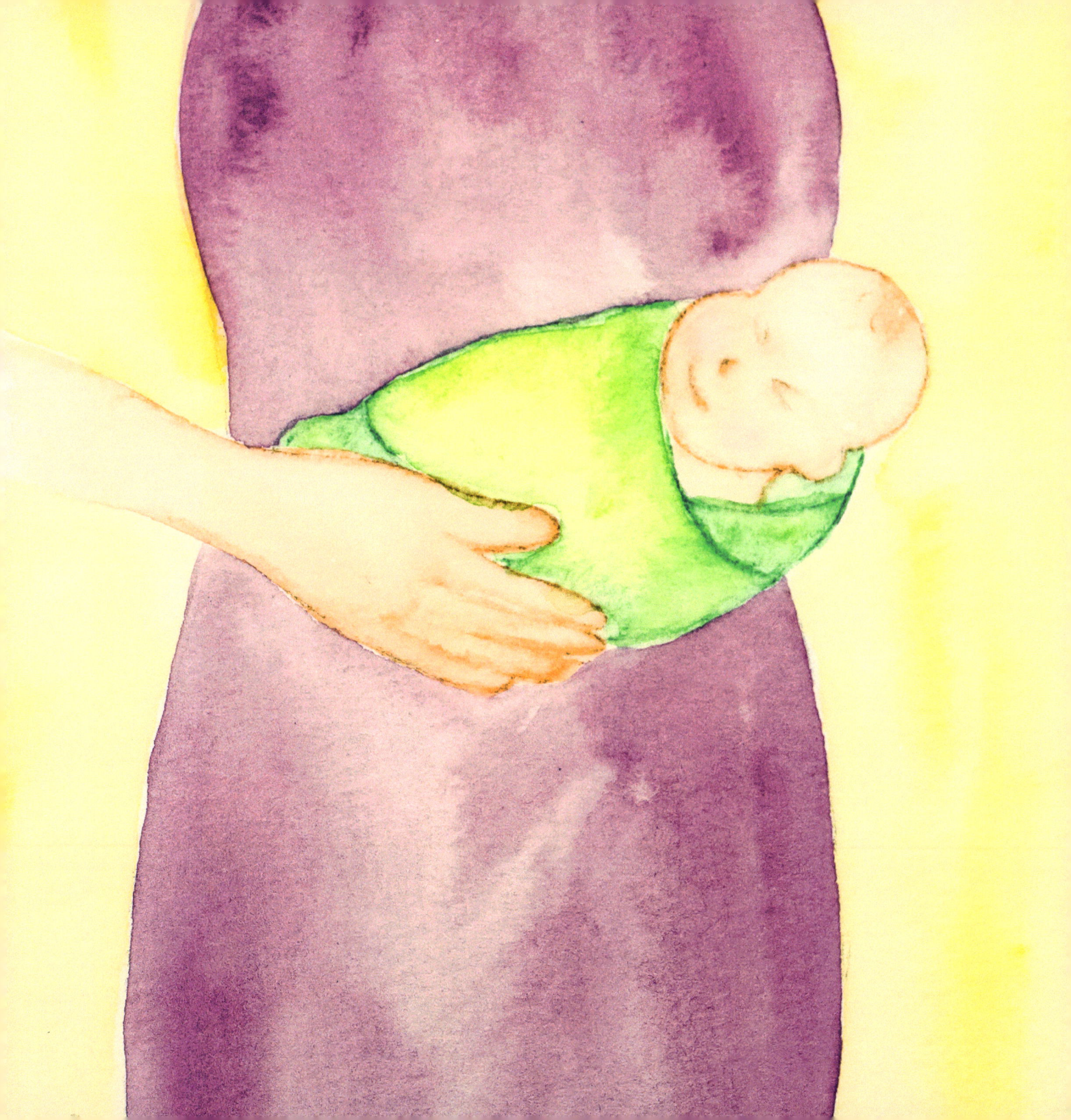

4 weeks

7 weeks

19 weeks

20 weeks

39 weeks

Newborn

About the Author

Amy is a full-time wife and mom of two toddlers, as well as a part-time freelance photographer. Her desire was to write a children's book that spoke to mothers about their journey through pregnancy and remind them of the beauty of becoming a mother while teaching children how babies grow.

Book Summary

Becoming a mother is a beautiful journey. From the excitement of the pregnancy news to feeling those first kicks, or holding your baby for the first time, there are precious memories in every moment. The author documents this experience through letters to her child.

Follow her on this journey while teaching kids how babies grow.

www.ingramcontent.com/pod-product-compliance
Lightning Source LLC
Chambersburg PA
CBHW041224040426

42443CB00002B/82